At Issue

| Cyberpredators

Other Books in the At Issue Series:

At Issue

I Cyberpredators

Stefan Kiesbye, Book Editor

GREENHAVEN PRESS
A part of Gale, Cengage Learning

GALE
CENGAGE Learning·

Detroit • New York • San Francisco • New Haven, Conn • Waterville, Maine • London

Elizabeth Des Chenes, *Managing Editor*

© 2012 Greenhaven Press, a part of Gale, Cengage Learning.

Gale and Greenhaven Press are registered trademarks used herein under license.

For more information, contact:
Greenhaven Press
27500 Drake Rd.
Farmington Hills, MI 48331-3535
Or you can visit our Internet site at gale.cengage.com

For product information and technology assistance, contact us at

Gale Customer Support, 1-800-877-4253
For permission to use material from this text or product, submit all requests online at www.cengage.com/permissions

Further permissions questions can be e-mailed to permissionrequest@cengage.com

Articles in Greenhaven Press anthologies are often edited for length to meet page requirements. In addition, original titles of these works are changed to clearly present the main thesis and to explicitly indicate the author's opinion. Every effort is made to ensure that Greenhaven Press accurately reflects the original intent of the authors. Every effort has been made to trace the owners of copyrighted material.

Cover image Illustration Works.

LIBRARY OF CONGRESS CATALOGING-IN-PUBLICATION DATA

Cyberpredators / Stefan Kiesbye, book editor.
    p. cm. -- (At issue)
    Includes bibliographical references and index.
    ISBN 978-0-7377-5564-0 (hardcover) -- ISBN 978-0-7377-5565-7 (pbk.)
    1. Online sexual predators. 2. Computer crimes. I. Kiesbye, Stefan.
    HV6773.15.O58C93 2012
    364.15'3--dc23
                                                    2011038122

Printed in the United States of America
    1 2 3 4 5   16 15 14 13 12

FD055

Contents

Introduction

On its website, the Federal Bureau of Investigation (FBI) warns that, "[t]here are individuals who attempt to sexually exploit children through the use of on-line services and the Internet. Some of these individuals gradually seduce their targets through the use of attention, affection, kindness, and even gifts. These individuals are often willing to devote considerable amounts of time, money, and energy in this process. They listen to and empathize with the problems of children. They will be aware of the latest music, hobbies, and interests of children. These individuals attempt to gradually lower children's inhibitions by slowly introducing sexual context and content into their conversations."

It is these predators that Detective Chris Bosley tries to locate before they can strike and harm unsuspecting children and teenagers. "I don't talk to my family about what I do," he said to reporter Susan Weich. "They just know that I arrest monsters." In an article on STLToday.com from February 23, 2011, Weich chronicles Bosley's line of police work—catching online predators. "Bosley actually has five different personas online. One of them is a teenage boy, although most of the people he encounters seeking sex on the Internet are heterosexual men, . . . He keeps cheat sheets handy for quick reference about clothes sizes or any other questions he may get, including bras and birth control. 'Sometimes if I can't find the sheet, I have to scream across the room to figure out what size clothes I wear.'"

Bosley's work is paid for by "local, state and federal grants as well as a budget from the St. Charles County Sheriff's Department in Missouri. Drug forfeiture money has also been used to buy equipment, such as a mobile cyber lab, a van where computers and other electronic devices can be evaluated."

Yet the type of work Bosley and his colleagues do has a high price tag. The *Appleton Post-Crescent*'s Andy Thompson writes that, "the volume of illegal online activity places a strain on the resources of state and local investigators." One of the officers interviewed for Thompson's article from August 15, 2011, confides that, "the advancements in technology also have allowed predators to do their job better. Every time a new cell phone comes out or the next generation of laptops comes out, any updated technology is something we need to be aware of and stay on top of. We struggle to keep up with the technology to make sure our agents have the training and experience to investigate crimes in certain venues." In addition, explains Cory McKone, a crime prevention officer at the Neenah Police Department in Wisconsin, "[T]he emergence of social networking sites and cell phone advances have complicated matters for investigators. . . . [Y]ou add . . . Facebook, Twitter and MySpace, and you've grouped a bunch of people together. You have these dedicated sites where kids post pictures and information about themselves."

As a result, police officers' attempts at weeding out cyberpredators have come under intense scrutiny from citizens and legislators who doubt that the high costs of catching online offenders are worthwhile, or who believe that the danger of online sexual offenders has been overblown. And if catching cyberpredators is expensive, dealing with criminals can seem financially overwhelming. Initiatives to deal with sexual offenders have drawn the ire of state and federal lawmakers. In Minnesota, "lawmakers are confronting the spiraling price of confining the state's most dangerous sex offenders after prison by sticking county governments with some of the tab," reports the *Associated Press*' Martiga Lohn. The treatment program is seen as too expensive, and legislators are pushing to find less costly ways to deal with sex offenders. In Texas, a proposed national sex offender registry has come under fire. According to a February 2011 article by Heather Caygle of the *Houston*

Chronicle, "[t]he state—which has the second-largest sex of-fender database in the nation, with 63,000 men and women registered—is balking at the law's requirements, citing unac-ceptably high costs of implementing the law's provisions."

Whether or not local and state governments will pay to catch and address the problem of cyberpredators depends on how society evaluates the danger. Has the danger posed by cy-berpredators been exaggerated by media outlets hungry for a good story, or is the risk posed by online sexual offenders to Internet-browsing teenagers as pervasive as some advocacy groups and concerned parents have made it out to be?

At Issue: Cyberpredators explores the dangers of online communications, and the different views on the impact of the Internet, social networking, chat rooms, and cyberbullying. It discusses parents' and guardians' fears, the new ways of com-munication open to teenagers and sexual offenders, and the possible need to craft new laws in an age when emerging tech-nologies are changing our culture at an ever increasing rate.

1

Online Sexual Exploitation Is a Serious Problem

Jilliane Hoffman

Jilliane Hoffman worked as an assistant state attorney in Florida from 1992 to 1996, focusing on prosecuting felonies with special assignments to the Domestic Violence Unit and the Legal Extradition Unit. She has also authored novels, including Last Witness *and* Pretty Little Things.

Social networking sites attract many registered sex offenders, who pose a grave danger to kids and teenagers. Sex offenders groom unsuspecting youth, then encourage real-life meetings, often with tragic consequences. To keep children safe, parents must monitor their children's computer and networking habits carefully, and they must be taught about potential online threats.

Last December [2009], New York's Attorney General Andrew Cuomo announced that more than 3500 registered sex offenders had been purged from the social networking sites Facebook and MySpace in the state's first database sweep for sexual predators.

That's 3500 caught, convicted and registered sex offenders who'd actually used their real names when they signed up for a Facebook or MySpace page. That's not counting all the deviants that haven't yet been busted, pled to a lesser charge, had charges dropped, never registered their emails with their probation or parole officers, socially communicate using an alias, or live outside the Empire State. With that in mind, consider this sobering statistic: According to the Center for Sex Offender Management (CSOM), the average sex offender offends for 16 years before he's finally caught. In that time span, he has committed an average of 318 offenses and violated 110 victims.

The explosion of the Internet over the past decade has spawned fertile hunting grounds for sex offenders.

Wow. Now just imagine who your kids may be chatting with online.

Hunting for Friends

The explosion of the Internet over the past decade has spawned fertile hunting grounds for sex offenders. Kids, and particularly teens, live their lives instantaneously and out loud on social networks, where every detail from where they'll be hanging out that night to who they'll be with and what they'll be wearing when they get there is posted for all of their "friends" to see. And those friends are not just the traditional bunch of kids you've known since elementary school.

Social networking sites and chat rooms have literally opened up a whole new cyber-world to children. Online, they can be "friends" with hundreds, sometimes thousands, of people from all over the globe, most of whom they've never met outside of a WiFi connection. And of course, as the tragic headlines constantly remind us, in this faceless cyber world not everything is kid-friendly and not everyone is who they say they are.

There are over 665,000 registered convicted sex offenders living in the United States. According to a study commissioned by the National Center for Missing and Exploited Children, one in every seven kids has been approached by a sexual predator online. That's 13% of children who use the Internet.

Sex Offenders no longer need to leave the comfort of their living rooms to find and "groom" fresh victims. Rather, with just the click of a mouse, they can mingle in chatrooms, send and receive child pornography, and, of course, purview the walls of Facebook and the posts of MySpace like they might entrees on a dinner menu, replete with helpful personal information and pictures.

Kids Making Questionable Decisions

Just ask the detectives who work online undercover or the producers of *Dateline*'s popular "To Catch a Predator"—in this fast-moving cyberworld, a predator can be anyone he wants to be: A twelve year-old boy, Jay-Z's agent, a modeling scout, a fourteen year-old girl. And teens, being the invincible bunch they are, always believe they'll be able to spot a poser or a predator a mile off on the computer, when the truth is they can't—oftentimes until it is way too late. They've already been groomed.

Back in the mid 90's, in response to the headline-making abduction of eleven year-old Jacob Wetterling of Wisconsin, and the sexual assault and murder of seven year-old Megan Kanka by her neighbor, a repeat child sex offender in New Jersey, the feds enacted a series of laws designed to warn the public of the presence of dangerous sex offenders and heighten community awareness on an issue that was literally moving in right next door to Joe the Plumber.

Each state was charged with establishing a sex offender registry and implementing a community notification program. The theory behind which was simple: Knowledge is power. If a sex offender is going to be out and about in the community, people—and more particularly, parents—should arm themselves with information about their identities and whereabouts so as to better protect their kids. Without promoting vigilantism, making yourself aware of the scum living in your zip code that your children might very well come in contact with and warning kids appropriately can be a very effective crime-fighting tool. But in today's world, where every kid has a cell phone in their pocket and a computer in their room, it's just not enough.

Predators Put Children at Risk Online

My daughter was in the fourth grade when a fellow eleven year-old classmate was approached on AIM (AOL Instant Messenger) by a 43 year-old sexual predator who went by the screen name of "rooster69" and claimed he was a 16 year-old boy. It wasn't until he asked one of the little girl's friends to send him nude pictures that one of the children finally spoke up. I thought I had more time to ready myself on the dangers of the Internet. I was wrong.

[A]s a parent you have to know of what you speak. So if you don't have a Facebook or MySpace yourself, you better thoroughly check it out.

So what's a parent to do? How can you make sure your kids are Facebooking with fellow thirteen year olds and not forty-three-year-old convicted sex offenders? I'm a big believer in the real world. Show kids the headlines. Let them read the stories of teens who disappeared or were assaulted after meeting up with someone they met online. The stories are out there, and there are plenty of them. . . .

Then talk to your kids about limiting the amount of personal information they post, particularly addresses and schedules; inappropriate posts and pictures; the new horrible growing fad of sexting; and finally, limiting the amount of "friends" they have and just what those friends are able to see. And as a parent you have to know of what you speak. So if you don't have a Facebook or MySpace yourself, you better thoroughly check it out. And if you do allow your kid access to a social network, it should be a number one rule that he or she "friends" you with unrestricted access, so that you can monitor what he or she is doing.

Then make sure you do just that.

2

The Dangers of Online Sexual Exploitation Have Been Exaggerated

Lenore Skenazy

Lenore Skenazy is founder of freerangekids.com, a website devoted to raising children without becoming an overprotective parent. She is also the author of Free-Range Kids: Giving Our Children the Freedom We Had Without Going Nuts with Worry.

News about cyberpredators has many parents worried about the online safety of their kids. But reports about incidents of sexual harassment and abuse have been misinterpreted and have overstated the potential dangers of social networking sites and texting. If parents explain safe Internet use to their children and educate them about responsible communication of personal data, the instances of kids and teenagers being molested by people they met online can be reduced significantly.

Is letting your kids go online the same as dropping them off at the Vince Lombardi Rest Stop in fishnet stockings at 3 a.m.?

A lot of parents think it is. Or maybe worse. My husband and I took our time letting our oldest boy, who is 13, start his social networking, though that was because we were worried it was like dropping him off at the Vince Lombardi Rest Stop to do his homework—we figured it would never get done. But the towering fear that the second a kid goes online he or she becomes cyberjailbait turns out to be way off base. According to new research, the danger online is teeny-tiny unless your kids are running into chat rooms, typing, "Anyone here like 'em young?" and posting photos of themselves licking lolli-pops. Naked.

Fears Are Blown out of Proportion

"The notion that predators are using the Internet as an L.L. Bean catalog, that's not what's happening," says the study's author.

That reassuring fact comes from a man who studies child predators for a living: David Finkelhor, head of the Crimes Against Children Research Center at the University of New Hampshire. He's the one responsible for the terrifying statistic, "One in seven juveniles will be solicited online"—a number that got predictably huge media play when it came out in 2006, and a number he stands by, with one enormous caveat: Most of those solicitations, he says, are the Internet equivalent of "wolf whistles." In other words, they come from guys who are drive-by typing, saying things like, "What's your bra size?" and "Are you a virgin?" Not guys actually trying to lure *Dora the Explorer* fans off to the mall.

All new technologies freak us out.

As uncomfortable as these comments might make us feel as parents, they're absolutely nothing new. Do your children leave the house occasionally? Then they've probably heard similar comments many times before. The reason this type of lechery gets so much attention when it happens online, Finkel-hor believes, is that it serves as "revealing ink"—typed out, visible evidence of something that has always gone on, more or less unnoticed. "So, for example," says Finkelhor, "when your daughter is walking to school with her friend, you don't see every motorist who leers at them." On the Internet, you do, because the leering appears as words on a screen. This makes the hoots and hollers seem more menacing. But are they evidence that online child predators are a big threat?

Finkelhor's whole motive in life is to keep kids safe from sexual predators. That's why he doesn't want people focusing on the wrong thing—unlikely scenarios like cyberstalking—when there are bigger dangers, like sex abuse in the home. To keep things in perspective, he studies our worst fears to separate the real from the urban myth. His earlier revelations about the rarity of sensationalized kidnappings—the kind you see on *Nancy Grace*—made people realize (some people, anyway) that our kids really are not in much danger just walking down the street. Their chances of being abducted and killed by a stranger are, according to the numbers he crunched, 1 in 1.5 million. That's about 50 children a year—a statistic it makes my stomach sink to write—but far less than the 1,000 killed each year by relatives or acquaintances, a far more stomach-sinking stat.

The Fear of New Technologies

More recently, Finkelhor turned his attention to the Internet predator, because that's our newest boogeyman. It almost had to be. All new technologies freak us out. When telegrams came along, people worried that telegraph poles were going to screw up worldwide weather patterns. (Hmmm.) But the truth about cyberstalking? Earlier this month, Finkelhor and his colleague Janis Wolak released a new study of the number of online predators arrested from 2000 to 2006. The results?

NUMBER OF ONLINE PREDATOR ARRESTS SKY-ROCKETING!

That's how I expect it will be repeated at PTA [Parent Teacher Association] meetings from here till eternity, anyway. But the news as the Crimes Against Children Research Center sees it is this: "The facts do not suggest that the Internet is facilitating an epidemic of sex crimes against youth," says the report.

The issue isn't whether there are dangerous people online. Of course there are. Almost everyone *is online.*

While the number of arrests did indeed shoot up, from 1,152 to 3,744, the vast majority of the perps pulled in (3,100) were arrested for soliciting the increasing number of law-enforcement decoys—cops online pretending to be juveniles. These decoys skew the numbers upward because they aggressively court potential molesters, a lot more than your average teen ever would.

Now, you might argue that it doesn't matter if the cops are all but prancing around in their skivvies to get the molesters to act—if act they do, then they're predators who ought to be locked up. But that misses the point. The issue isn't whether there are dangerous people online. Of course there are. Almost *everyone* is online. The issue is whether the online world is any more dangerous than the real world, and according to Finkelhor, it's not.

Which is probably why arrests of creeps soliciting *actual* youths totaled only 614. That's up just 21 percent in the six years of the study. During that same period, Internet use among juveniles rose from 73 percent of the population to 93 percent. In other words, millions of people under age 18 joined the online world, and 107 more creeps were arrested for soliciting them. That number may still seem appalling, but generally it does not even represent fiendish strangers luring unsuspecting children into sex.

The Image of Sexual Predators Has Been Distorted

In the cases where a minor does end up in a sexual scenario with someone too old for them, usually that someone isn't decades older—a 21-year-old chatting with a 16-year-old, for example—and both parties make their intentions very clear. This is a far cry from most parents' fear that posting a picture of cheerleading practice might be enough to bring on the Humbert Humberts [characters in Vladimir Nabokov's "Lolita"].

"The notion that predators are using the Internet as an L.L. Bean catalog, that's not what's happening," said Finkelhor. "That's a very low-yield strategy for them." Perverts trolling for cute kids on My Space would have about as much luck dialing numbers out of the phone book and asking for a date. It just doesn't work and they know it.

So instead they go looking for "low-hanging fruit. Kids who are going to be easy. And they do that much more by going to places where there's already a kind of hint of sexual availability," says Finkelhor.

Perverts trolling for cute kids on MySpace would have about as much luck dialing numbers out of the phone book and asking for a date.

Thus, skeeves tend to gravitate toward chat rooms geared to sexual topics like dating and romance, and sometimes to support groups for sexual minorities. In other words: Not Club Penguin. And not your kid's Facebook page.

Still, on one of many Web sites devoted to childhood safety (this one called "Connect With Kids"), a police officer compares the dangers of the Internet to the real world thusly: "I can tell you, it's like going to a big, empty field and putting a big plate of ice cream on a blanket and walking away for an hour and coming back and finding out how many ants and flies there are, because that's what it's like. It's almost unbelievable how many people are out there, every day, searching in chat rooms for children."

Responsible Internet Use Is Safe for Kids

He's right—if by "big plate of ice cream" he means a cop decoy wandering into a sexually charged chat room and hinting that she (or he) is horny as heck and sweet 16 and her parents are out of town and gee she'd like an iPod and a backrub.

Nothing is ever 100 percent safe—a fact a lot of us have forgotten.

In other words, if she drops herself off at the Vince Lombardi Rest Stop in fishnet stockings.

My 13-year-old is online and I'm not worried. We've talked (and talked!) about relationships, safety, sex, integrity, and the unlikelihood that anyone would give him an iPod, or anything, for free. Our job as parents is to prepare kids, not to lock them away from technology.

Nothing is ever 100 percent safe—a fact a lot of us have forgotten. But when you do remember this, the Internet seems less like a truck stop after dark, and more like the rest of the world: a reasonable place our kids can hang out with each other.

After they've done their homework.

3

Children on the Internet Are Prey for Cyberpredators

Chris Hopkins

Chris Hopkins is a Special Agent with the Federal Bureau of Investigation (FBI) and has worked on hundreds of cases involving children. He wrote the e-book The Internet Got My Baby *to help prevent future crimes involving online predators.*

Teenagers often make impulsive and unwise decisions, and the rise of the Internet has helped to exacerbate the dangers stemming from these ill-informed decisions. Through social networking sites and new technology, children are accessible to sex offenders around the globe; and child pornography has been made available to everyone who searches for it. Many pedophiles and other sexual offenders are using the Internet to "groom" children—to win their trust and make them record nude pictures of themselves, or to meet them in person. And while sex offenders have always preyed on unsuspecting children, the Internet gives them ample new opportunities to approach teenagers in secret. To insure teenagers' safety, parents have the obligation to capture and review their children's online information, as well as to discuss it with them.

In order to understand children's and teens' susceptibility to online dangers, one must understand the child's mind. Children and teens do not yet possess the mental tools they need to recognize online dangers and make good, safe decisions online. This is just part of the natural brain development and maturation process.

Kids and teens can be impulsive, rebellious, irritable, un-communicative, friend-oriented, risk-takers, and sleep-deprived. At any time they can be suffering from one of these conditions, several of these conditions, or worst-case scenario, all of these conditions. Remember, at any given time, your child may be in the perfect storm to be susceptible to one of the many online dangers. Kids believe they will never become a victim. They recognize that kids do become victims, how-ever, they do not believe they will fall prey to any attack or an online danger. Often, kids do not consider the consequence of their actions before they take great risks.

Their brains are truly "a work in progress" and one of the last areas of the brain to mature is the prefrontal cortex. The prefrontal cortex is responsible for processing information, making judgments, controlling impulses, and foreseeing con-sequences. If you compare the functions of the prefrontal cor-tex with the list of teen behaviors and conditions listed in the above paragraph, it is easy to recognize and understand teen behavior. Keep in mind that the brain does not typically reach full maturity until the age of 25. . . .

Keep in mind that the brain does not typically reach full maturity until the age of 25.

Online Sexual Offenders

Years ago, a small group of preferential sexual predators made a very short video called "Chicken Hawk." The content of the video is an alarming claim/threat made by them to all parents. The basic message in the video is, ". . . we will get your chil-dren and there is nothing you can do to stop us."

This is such an outrageous threat and yet, I believe their motive is true. Knowing their commitment and their selfish preferential sexual drive, we must all pull together to stand strong and not allow the enemy in.

Online sexual offenders get a lot of attention for all the right reasons. These people prey on our children to satisfy their sexual fantasy. Sometimes, if successful, these encounters can be absolutely catastrophic, if not deadly. The psychological trauma suffered by children that have been sexually assaulted can last for years.

Before the Internet, sexual offenders would put themselves in positions so they could have legitimate contact with children. They would use these positions to build trust and gain influence over children in order to execute their sexual fantasy. This process is referred to as grooming. Most often, the grooming process is subtle, occurs over a period of time, and your child is usually not aware that it is happening.

"Grooming" Teenagers and Kids

With respect to the Internet, we need to segregate sexual offenders into two categories. The first category includes family members and acquaintances, or non-stranger sexual offenders. This category is often overlooked during discussions of online sexual predators. However, family members and acquaintances often use the Internet to aid them in achieving their sexual fantasy. The second category is stranger offenders. These offenders are unknown to the victim and they use the Internet initially to gain access to their intended targets.

The psychological trauma suffered by children that have been sexually assaulted can last for years.

Although the statistics vary among studies regarding sex crimes against children, they all conclude that children are much more likely to be sexually assaulted by an acquaintance or a family member, than by a stranger, with the range being between 70 to 90 percent.

The Internet often plays a facilitative role in acquaintance or family member sexual abuse cases against children. These non-stranger offenders will use the Internet to build trust with their intended victim. This trust building process is very similar to the grooming process used by online predators. However, the non-stranger offender has a significant advantage over the stranger offender because the non-stranger offender has a preexisting baseline of trust.

Most parents and guardians often have a "weird" feeling about some relative or acquaintance (teacher, coach, neighbor, etc.). Family member or acquaintance offenders will use the Internet to communicate with the victims outside the parents' presence. This communication allows them to build a level of trust that will allow them to initiate sexual conversations and share sexual images. Non-stranger offenders would not be successful hiding their communications with kids if our solution was in place. The communications would be captured (part I) and the parent would recognize the inappropriate sexual overtures (part II). With this information, the parent could initiate the appropriate conversation with their child (part III).

Due to the overwhelming success of the Internet, predators can now engage hundreds of kids on a daily basis.

Child Pornography

Non-stranger sexual offenders will also use the Internet to share and trade with other sexual predators child pornography images they have captured. Sometimes they capture these images in a covert manner. On other occasions, they manipulate the victim to pose for pictures or manipulate the victim to take their own pictures. Acquaintance or family member offenders have even been known to sell their victims for sex. Many times, as a result, teens run away from home and resort to prostitution in order to survive. In order to protect our children, parents, foster parents, and guardians need to be vigilant concerning the various ways the Internet can be used to promote teen prostitution.

With the advent of the Internet, stranger sexual offenders can now disguise themselves and go to chat rooms, social networking sites (e.g., MySpace, Facebook, Xanga, Bebo, MyYearbook, WePlay), online gaming sites, or any place they believe their intended victims are present. This is done with the same intended purpose: to groom and gain influence over children. Due to the overwhelming success of the Internet, predators can now engage hundreds of kids on a daily basis. This is an absolutely frightening fact.

The National Center for Missing and Exploited Children (NCMEC) website states that:

- Only 42% of the children reported distress encounters—episodes that made them feel very or extremely upset or afraid—to a parent or guardian.

- 34% of the kids had unwanted exposure to sexual material.

- Only 27% of the children reported unwanted sexual exposure to a parent or guardian.

- 14% of children between the ages of 10 and 17 have received sexual solicitation or have been approached online.

- 4% of these kids received an aggressive sexual solicitation to meet someone, speak on the telephone, or receive mail, money or a gift.

Sexual Solicitations

The statistics reported by NCMEC are staggering. It has been my experience, and the experience of my FBI [Federal Bureau of Investigation] partners, that the real numbers associated with online sexual solicitation is much higher. This is not sur-

prising considering the overwhelming number of sexual offenders that use the Internet to engage with children on a
daily basis. Just as alarming as the amount of unwanted exposure to sexual material, is the fact that most kids are not reporting inappropriate sexual contact to parents or guardians.
This is why I believe the number of online sexual solicitations
is much higher. And sadly, kids are trying to deal with this
sort of contact by themselves or with their peers.

The *Journal of Adolescent Health*, 2004, reported that 76%
of the victims in Internet initiated exploitation cases were 13
to 15 years old and 75% were girls. "Most cases progressed to
sexual encounters."

Researchers from the Crimes Against Children Research
Center, at the University of New Hampshire, reported in 2008
the following information concerning online predators:

- They are looking for teenagers.

- They are adult men who are honest about their age and
  about being online in search of sex.

- They don't pretend to be another kid or teen (5% pose
  as a youth).

- They often take their time establishing teenagers' trust
  (grooming behavior) through emails, chat rooms, and
  instant messaging in order to seduce or romance them
  into having intimate relationships that will lead to sex.

The same research group reported the following about the
kids who are targeted by these Internet predators:

- They usually know they are communicating with an
  adult online.

- They say they love or have strong feelings for the adult
  sex offenders.

- They often see the online sex offender face-to-face re-
  peatedly (nearly three-quarters of the kids who end up

meeting the adult sex offenders get together with them more than once and many meet fully expecting some sort of sexual encounter).

- They are most often girls, though almost a quarter of the victims in criminal Internet sex offender cases are boys.

- They are more vulnerable to "aggressive sexual solicitations" when they:

  talk to strangers online about sex;

  keep instant messaging "buddy lists" that include people they don't know;

  are "rude or nasty online";

  have a history of: abuse (physical or sexual), problems at home (including strained relationships with parents), depression, and/or risk-taking behaviors not only on the Internet but in the real world.

The problem of sexual offenders online is not limited to the United States. The Internet has no boundaries, thus predators from around the world have access to our children.

Drawbacks of the Internet

MySpace has reported publicly that they cannot police their website. In addition, The Canadian Safety Council writes, "the unregulated environment of cyberspace is virtually impossible to police." MySpace reported in February 2009 that 90,000 (that is not a typo) registered sex offenders have been kicked off of their site in the past two years! Ninety thousand registered sex offenders! The number is staggering and don't think for one minute that MySpace has identified all of the sex offenders on their site. These sexual offenders are only those registered in the United States. Other sexual offenders not registered in the United States or living in another country are still on MySpace. These 90,000 registered sex offenders removed by MySpace most likely have profiles on other social networking sites.

The problem of sexual offenders online is not limited to the United States. The Internet has no boundaries, thus predators from around the world have access to our children. You might think that your children are safe from predators from other countries. The prevailing thought is that it would be very unlikely that a predator from another country would travel to the United States to abduct or sexually assault my child. The fact is that the predator does not have to leave his country to sexually exploit your child.

There are many ways sexual predators can sexually exploit children without ever having any actual physical contact with your child. There are many cases in which a predator has successfully gained control over a child through the Internet and made them take nude photographs or videos of themselves and send the images back to the predator. Or the predator may entice/coerce the child to engage in cybersex or phone sex.

Nonphysical Abuse

Predators will set up fictitious profiles with misleading domain names or user names. Predators lie about their age, sex, where they live, go to school and work, and any other characteristic that helps them engage with their intended target. They will post pictures that falsely represent their life, family, and friends. They are experts in gaining emotional bonds to kids. They share fictitious stories and offer empathy to ingratiate themselves to their intended target.

We have had numerous cases in which family members bring their daughters to the FBI Field Office and we expose their online boyfriend's true identity. Typically, the girls refuse to believe the true identity. Once they understand they have been deceived, the girls will often rationalize the offender's intent to lie. And we must understand that the kids are not at fault. It is just a great example of how much time the offender has spent in grooming the child and how successful they have been.

In order to prevent online predators from gaining influence over our kids, we must know whom our kids are talking to (part I of the solution). Very often, sexual online predators are very upfront about their potential sexual interest. But, they will not initially discuss the extent of their true sexual fantasy because it would be too frightening to the kids. However, they will engage the kids in sexual overtones and sexual innuendoes. This type of conversation is easy to detect and analyze (part II). Once armed with this information, the parent is ready to have the appropriate conversation with their child (part III).

As of 2009, Facebook has identified 8,487 registered sex offenders.

The Dangers of Social Networking

Recently, we took three groups of parents with kids that use the Internet, and asked them a series of questions. We asked them to express their opinions about MySpace. I was shocked to see such a universal negative response. MySpace was called "evil" and "dangerous." However, even with those very strong negative feelings, most of the kids were allowed to have MySpace accounts. Some parents said they monitored their kids while they were on MySpace.

Facebook has an estimated 500 million active users (twice the size as MySpace). Fifty percent of the active users log on to Facebook each day. The average account has 130 friends and people spend over 500 billion minutes per month on Facebook. Approximately 70% of the Facebook users are outside the United States. There are more than 100 million active Facebook users currently accessing Facebook through their mobile devices. People that use Facebook through their mobile devices are twice as active on Facebook than non-mobile users.

Facebook has not been as successful as MySpace at identifying registered sex offenders that have active profiles on their site. As of 2009, Facebook has identified 8,487 registered sex offenders. Again, sex offenders will often use fictitious names, ages, email addresses, IM addresses, and street addresses in an attempt to go undetected. They will also use a different picture to further cloak their true identity.

The security departments at MySpace and Facebook are working with a database of more than 700,000 registered sex offenders in the United States. But, I must remind you that there are thousands of sex offenders that are not registered in the United States. And when we are dealing with the Internet, we cannot just think about the United States, we need to think about the entire world population.

Sex Offenders Work Internationally

Sex offenders will go wherever kids go. Sex offenders will try to put themselves in legitimate environments that are populated by kids. So it only makes sense that social networking sites are populated with sex offenders, especially sites that are designed and marketed towards kids. In terms of kid-friendly environments, these sites are analogous to playgrounds. California is trying to pass a law that prohibits registered sex offenders from using any social networking site. By law, sex offenders in California are already restricted from going to places like schools and parks so it makes sense to extrapolate the law to social networking sites.

The case of Peter Chapman illustrates how sex offenders will hide their true identity and use social networking sites to lure their victims. Chapman was a 33 year-old sex offender that used a fictitious name and claimed to be a 17 year-old boy on Facebook. His Facebook profile attracted more than 14,600 visitors, and approximately 3,000 became online friends. All of his Facebook "friends" were girls ranging in age from 13 to 31.

Once they became his friend on Facebook, he would try to redirect them to private online chat rooms where he would invite them to provide sexually explicit details about themselves. One of Chapman's Facebook friends was a 17 year-old girl named Ashleigh Hall. Chapman used Facebook as a tool to groom Ashleigh. Unfortunately for Ashleigh, she had no idea she was communicating with a sexual monster. Chapman kidnapped, raped, and murdered Ashleigh. Chapman was convicted of these crimes and is now serving a life sentence in prison.

Criminals Use Many Disguises

The dangers of social networking sites are not limited to sex offenders. A Wisconsin teenager was convicted of using Facebook to blackmail dozens of classmates into having sex with him. He was sentenced to 15 years in prison for actions perpetrated against his classmates. . . .

Jill Tucker wrote a story in August 2009 for the *San Francisco Chronicle* titled, "Social networking has Hidden Dangers for Teens." The story was largely based on a study that was commissioned by Common Sense Media. Here are the results after surveying 1,000 teenagers:

- 51% checked their sites more than once a day.

- 22% checked their sites more than 10 times a day.

- 39% have posted something they later regretted.

- 37% have used the sites to make fun of other students.

- 25% have created a profile with a false identity.

- 24% have hacked into someone else's social networking account.

- 13% have posted nude or seminude pictures or videos of themselves or others online.

Just as alarming as these numbers is the fact that parents are unaware of what their kids are doing online. The study highlighted this fact by demonstrating the huge discrepancy between the kids' actual online behavior and what the parents perceived was their kids' online behavior.

Social networking sites/technology did not create bad teen behavior. It is just another mechanism to express bad behavior.

Parents Need to Be Part of the Solution

Kids use social networking sites to communicate with one friend or multiple friends simultaneously. They share everything from common school assignments to very personal information such as love, sex, pregnancy, substance abuse, smoking, anorexia, and bulimia. Our kids are dealing with very personal, sensitive, and complicated issues. We must strike a balance between their privacy and helping them navigate through these issues.

The information on the social networking sites must be captured and reviewed by a parent or guardian (part I and part II). The parent or guardian now has information that will allow them to discuss that information with their child (part III). And . . . research results clearly demonstrate, communication will lead to a decrease in high-risk behavior. . . .

Social networking sites are important to many of our kids because they provide information, support, and a sense of community. They are not the root of all evil, however, they provide an environment for abuse and destructive behavior. It is the underlying teen behaviors that need to be addressed. Social networking sites/technology did not create bad teen behavior. It is just another mechanism to express bad behavior. If parents are aware of these problems, they can help their kids with their issues.

4

The Benefits of Using Social Networking Sites in Class Outweigh the Risks

Nicholas Bramble

Nicholas Bramble is the Director of the Law and Media Program at the Information Society Project, and a lecturer at Yale Law School. He is a graduate of Stanford University and Harvard Law School, where he was the online managing editor of the Journal of Law & Technology.

Many schools have blocked social networking sites in an attempt to curb cyberbullying and the dissemination of risky pictures or student videos. However, integrating new technologies into the curriculum might be a more effective way to monitor students' online behavior and to insure that all teenagers are proficient and responsible Internet users. From working together on science to editing video, students should be encouraged by their teachers to utilize new media to advance students' knowledge and retain oversight.

At a suburban school district near Washington, D.C., the most popular teacher happens to be a local star on YouTube. Unbeknown to him, students with cell-phone cameras have videotaped him dancing to "Soulja Boy Tell 'Em" and other songs taught to him by the students.

Less sweetly, when another teacher from the same school Googled the school's name, she found videos showing students getting into fights with one another. They posted the videos to their MySpace pages and debated who had the better fighting skills. The teacher also found footage from a set of girls who had filmed themselves dancing suggestively in school stairwells. These videos were disturbing, inappropriate, and often exceptionally well-produced, with multiple camera angles and sophisticated editing cuts.

Unwanted Attention and Exposure

If the school administration knew of the videos, they would be deleted and the teenagers responsible for them would likely face suspensions—including the ones who taught their teacher how to dance to Soulja Boy. Schools have had a nearly unanimous response to Facebook, MySpace, and YouTube: repression and silence. Administrators block access to these sites because they think it's important to keep classrooms free from the perceived harms associated with social networks—harassment, bullying, exploitative advertising, violence, and sexual imagery.

But this is shortsighted. Educators should stop thinking about how to repress the huge amounts of intellectual and social energy kids devote to social media and start thinking about how to channel that energy away from causing trouble and toward getting more out of their classes. After all, it's not as if most kids are investing commensurate energy into, say, their math homework. Why not try to start bridging the worlds of Facebook, YouTube, and the classroom?

Schools have had a nearly unanimous response to Facebook, MySpace, and YouTube: repression and silence.

The main reason is fear. Megan Meier, the 13-year-old student in Missouri who committed suicide after an ex-friend's mother created a fake MySpace profile to humiliate her, stands as a warning against school involvement with the intricacies of kids' online social lives. In response to cyber-stalking and online solicitation of minors, the House of Representatives passed a bill in 2006—the Deleting Online Predators Act—that would require schools to block students from accessing sites like Facebook, MySpace, and LiveJournal. The Senate has put forward similar proposals. And even without a Congressional mandate, many schools have already taken the initiative to ban students—and teachers—from using these sites.

Block-Outs Are Not the Answer

Bad idea. Researchers have already enumerated the benefits that kids can get from traditional media. Watching Sesame Street or Blue's Clues improves children's problem-solving skills and school readiness. Teaching students how to use word-processing software, Web-design programs, and video-production tools is a proven way of refocusing at-risk teens on school, and, eventually, getting them jobs. Social networks can also pull in students who are otherwise disengaged, because they draw on kids' often intense interest in finding new ways to communicate with one another.

How can teachers bring social networking into the classroom? For starters, students could talk about what they're doing on Facebook and company, map out the ways they're making connections with one another, and share videos and software they've created. Once the conversation gets going, teachers could figure out whether some kids were being left out and find ways to increase those students' media literacy and bring them into the fold. Teachers can manage the project by selecting the best content and conversations, and incorporating it into other parts of the curriculum. If a student created an entry on Wikipedia for a local band or sports team, other students could work on revising the entry and building it into a larger local history project. The audience for school projects need no longer be one hurried teacher.

Schools could also find students like the ones who made the stairwell dance videos and get them to produce a school-sanctioned video with a better subject—the re-enactment of a literary or historical scene, for example. This isn't as simple as a teacher saying, "Why don't you write a poem about your frustration, rap it on video, and put it on YouTube?" Instead, a teacher could assign students the task of filming a scene from *The Scarlet Letter* in the stairwell, identifying the dynamic of shaming in the novel, and writing about how it might be playing out in their Facebook news feeds. In math class, students could develop statistical models and graphs of the patterns of information flow in their social networks. To understand how advertising works, students from different backgrounds and with different online habits could compare what's being hawked to them. And for a school journalism project, teams of students could aggregate other students' narratives from blogs, Facebook, and Twitter and compile a real-time collective analysis of the state of their educational union.

Social networks can also pull in students who are otherwise disengaged, because they draw on kids' often intense interest in finding new ways to communicate with one another.

Using the Internet as an Educational Tool

In the process, teachers could also gain technical skills and be in a better position to head off future online trouble. Consider this recent MySpace post from Washington, D.C.: "I swear man when I see Martin and Kris on the bus they going to get it, Trina u a snitch, me and Bobby going to beat the shit out of them" (names changed). A school psychologist who knew about it could talk to the kids involved in hopes of preventing a real-world fight.

Schools also stand to gain from harnessing students' budding tech expertise. Rather than relying on private companies like Blackboard for expensive software, schools can get students who are taking computer programming to develop social media tools, apps, and platforms for creating and sharing class projects. These projects could then go on a school's Web site, in an iTunes-style store. Moodle, Ck12.org, and Sakai are great examples of how schools are using this new kind of open, cost-effective learning.

But there are ways to discipline students other than through the typical punishment of suspension.

Some teachers and administrators might object that such proposals inadvertently reward students for online misbehavior. But there are ways to discipline students other than through the typical punishment of suspension. Editing videos is slow and painstaking; a student could be made to stay after school or miss a free period to work on it.

Another objection is that proposals like these break down the distinction between the schoolyard and the classroom, and could allow mean and anonymous student gossip to further invade children's lives. To be sure, the classroom does serve as a sanctuary, sometimes, from petty concerns and conflicts. But slamming the classroom door on social media just makes the virtual world more of a wasteland. A hundred years ago, John Dewey warned that when teachers suppress children's natural interests in the classroom, they "substitute the adult for the child, and so weaken intellectual curiosity and alertness, suppress initiative, and deaden interest." By locking social networking out of school, teachers and principals are making exactly that error. Instead, they should meet kids where they live: online.

5

An App Might Connect Children to Pornography or Predators

Joel Schectman

Joel Schectman is a reporter for Newsweek.

The porn industry is exploiting an iPhone 4 feature for its own purposes, using FaceTime videoconferencing to allow for sex chat on the mobile device. While porn producers see it as a new frontier of making money, parents are worried that online predators might appropriate the iPhone to harass children. Also, parents are no longer able to monitor their children's access to pornography and sexually explicit video chat.

It's a maxim of technology: Invent a gadget and the porn industry will find a way to cash in.

So when Apple Inc. launched the iPhone 4 and its FaceTime videoconference feature, it didn't take long for adult-entertainment companies to develop video-sex chat services and start hiring workers through Craigslist.

With more than 3 million of the phones already sold, the adult industry stands to make big money on this new way to reach out and touch someone—even if it puts Apple, which has always taken pains to keep its iPhone apps squeaky clean, in an awkward spot.

In at least five cities, Craigslist ads seek models specifically for video-sex chat on FaceTime. Many of the ads even offer to throw in a free iPhone 4 for the new employees.

FaceTime lets people call other iPhone 4 users and have live video conversations over a Wi-Fi connection using the front-facing camera on the new model. In one TV ad, a soldier uses it to get a look at his faraway wife's ultrasound pictures.

The adult industry wants its customers to share moments of an entirely different kind with its stars. And while the technology may be new, the idea is not. Porn providers have always been early adopters.

In at least five cities, Craigslist ads seek models specifically for video-sex chat on FaceTime.

In the 1970s, the demand for explicit videos at home helped VCRs become widespread, and the industry was the first to embrace DVDs, too. Internet porn peddlers were some of the first to make wide use of streaming video and online credit card payments.

"The first time someone created a camera there was someone who said, 'Wouldn't it be good for someone to take off their clothes in front of this camera?'" said Michael Gartenberg, vice president at Interpret LLC, a media research company.

New Frontier

And for years, cameras mounted on computers have helped connect people for racy online video sessions. But the portability and privacy of a cell phone makes FaceTime a new frontier for the industry.

"A phone is such an intimate thing, you usually don't lend it out or have someone else use it," said Quentin Boyer, a spokesman for Pink Visual, an adult production company.

Boyer said his company began planning for iPhone 4 video services almost as soon as the device hit stores. They should be ready in a matter of weeks. Boyer said the company will offer FaceTime sessions with some of the same women who appear in its videos—probably charging $5 or $6 a minute, payable by credit card.

So far, most online, video-sex chat services have let the customer see the performer, but not the other way around. FaceTime may change that.

"It has a very personal feel—your mobile phone to hers," he said.

Online exhibitionism is only growing. Take Chatroulette, which randomly connects strangers for video chats. While the service isn't explicitly sexual, it's common for users to stumble upon people looking for more than just conversation.

So far, most online, video-sex chat services have let the customer see the performer, but not the other way around. FaceTime may change that.

"We are seeing more and more that customers want to be watched as much as they want to watch," said Dan Hogue, owner of an adult chat company called CamWorld, which is planning FaceTime services.

The rise of FaceTime porn puts Apple in an awkward position. Its competitors have products that allow video chat, too—HTC's Evo 4G phone, for one. But Apple has made a big deal about keeping applications sold in its iTunes store clean.

Apple has rejected book apps for featuring sexual content and political satires for their potential to offend. Although some rejected apps have been approved after revisions, Apple has kept one strict rule: no porn.

FaceTime isn't even an outside developer's app. It's a main feature of the phone.

An e-mail attributed to CEO Steve Jobs that was posted on technology blogs in April says it is Apple's "moral responsibility" to keep pornography off the iPhone. Apple would not confirm that Jobs wrote it.

But just as Apple can't control whom iPhone users call, the company will have a hard time dictating how FaceTime is used. Internet experts say customers will understand that Apple cannot control what goes on in private video chats.

Parents can put computers in public areas of the home to supervise Internet usage, but mobile phones go anywhere.

"Apple can't be seen as responsible any more than makers of routers or hardware are responsible for the content you are looking at," said Jonathan Zittrain, a co-founder of the Berkman Center for Internet & Society at Harvard University.

Serious Concerns

Still, advocacy groups worry that FaceTime could connect children to pornography or predators. Parents can put computers in public areas of the home to supervise Internet usage, but mobile phones go anywhere.

"Unfortunately, both children and sexual predators are often ahead of parents when it comes to technology," says Donna Rice Hughes, president of Enough Is Enough, a child safety group.

Apple, asked to comment on the emerging adult services, noted that people can choose whom they chat with, just like regular calls, and parents can turn off the Face-Time feature. Hughes said it would be better if parents could create a "safe list" of people their children could call.

6

Education Is Key to Keeping Children Safe Online

Amanda Paulson

Amanda Paulson is an award-winning journalist and education reporter for the Christian Science Monitor.

In order to make children understand the possibly dangerous consequences of posting personal information online, parents need to take a proactive stance and educate their children about responsible Internet use. New technologies and mobile devices are here to stay, and teenagers are prone to making unwise and impulsive decisions, so parents cannot wait until it is too late. Instead, they should explain the threat of predators hunting for personal data and pictures, of cyberbullying, and what their teens can do to avoid tragic consequences.

For parents who worried about the potential dangers in new technology, and are unsure how to help their kids navigate a wireless world safely, there may be comfort in the basic message from a new guide from the Federal Trade Commission [FTC]: Talk to your kids.

Ultimately, simply addressing these issues with your kids—and emphasizing that the basic rules that guide communications offline are the same ones that should apply to communication online—is what's important, says Nat Wood, an assistant director in the FTC's Bureau of Consumer Protection.

"The reach of modern communication technology means it can be really hard to step away from a mistake, but the principals of communicating in a civil way are the same on-line and off," says Mr. Wood, who worked on the FTC guide, known as Net Cetera. "In a lot of ways, this makes it easier on parents."

Still, the combination of typical teenage poor judgment with the far reach of today's technology haunts many parents, who envision their teenagers being harassed by peers, stalked by a sexual predator, or answering questions from a potential boss or college admissions officer about the embarrassing photos they posted to their Facebook page.

"The reach of modern communication technology means it can be really hard to step away from a mistake, but the principals of communicating in a civil way are the same online and off. . . ."

Kids Sometimes Show Poor Judgment

Valerie, a mother in North Dakota who prefers not to use her last name because of privacy concerns, was surprised when her 16-year-old daughter's cell phone started registering a lot of odd numbers. She went onto Michelle's MySpace page—available to anyone—and discovered she'd posted her number, and many other private details, along with the message, "I'm bored, text me."

"I think we fell down on the job by not being more cautious and watching more," says Valerie, who talked to Michelle and showed her how much personal data came up simply through googling her phone number. "She nearly had a heart attack," says Valerie. "It was a huge wake-up call when she saw how much was out there about her."

Michelle and her parents worked together to come up with some acceptable guidelines—don't share passwords, don't post questionable photos or sensitive information such as phone numbers or hometown, don't list your age.

Valerie and her husband also made a rule that the family laptop can't be taken into the kids' bedrooms.

That story is a fairly typical one, internet-safety experts say: Kids don't mean to create problems, but often don't have the best judgment and don't think about the potential consequences.

But reacting too harshly—particularly by denying access to technology or using filters—is unlikely to work, and also denies the many positive aspects of new technology to increasingly-connected teenagers, they add.

"Teens whose parents are actively and positively involved in what their children are doing, both online and in the real world, are the ones who engage in less risky behavior online," says Nancy Willard, executive director of the Center for the Safe and Responsible Use of the Internet.

The biggest dangers kids face online are from peers who misuse information or harass others, or from their own poor judgment in posting images that later reach the wrong people.

Cyberpredators Are Not the Main Threat

She also cautions parents against being too paranoid. The cyber-predator threat that was hyped in much of the past decade is exceedingly rare, she notes. The biggest dangers kids face online are from peers who misuse information or harass others, or from their own poor judgment in posting images that later reach the wrong people.

"The entire conversation with young people has to be focused on 'What are the potential harmful consequences?'" Ms. Willard says. "It's not rule-based, it's consequence-based."

Larry Rosen, a professor of psychology at California State University in Dominguez Hills and author of "Me, MySpace and I," agrees, and says that a lot of the issues today come from parents who are happy to let their kids be occupied by technology but never actively talk about it with them.

Talking to kids proactively—perhaps using a news story to raise the issue—is key, says Professor Rosen. "They don't have the best decision-making abilities, and they're just kids," he says.

Those approaches are also emphasized in the FTC guide, which provides a glossary of terms and explicit information about cyber-bullying, sexting, file sharing, and other potential sources of problems. The guide also points to the positive elements of kids' online communication and advises parents to start discussions young and keep communication channels open.

Net Cetera, the guide, "is value-neutral and caters neither to the 'left' nor the 'right,' but it encourages parents to communicate their own values to their kids," Jon Leibowitz, the FTC chairman, said Wednesday in releasing the guide. "When parents are up front about their values and how they apply in the online world, kids will make more thoughtful decisions when they face tricky situations."

7

Gay Youth Are at a Greater Risk of Being Sexually Exploited

Bob Roehr

Bob Roehr is a biomedical writer based in Washington, DC. He has published articles in Scientific American, BMJ (British Medical Journal), Medscape, *and other publications.*

Gay youth are at a higher risk of falling victim to online-initiated sex crimes than their peers, partly because they are driven by stigma and bullying to explore their sexuality away from the public eye. While many crimes are committed by older offenders, they don't necessarily involve violence or force. Parents and schools can lessen the threat of online predators by openly discussing issues related to sexual orientation.

Youth who are gay or are questioning their sexual identity are significantly more likely than others to be victims of Internet-initiated sex crimes. However, the vast majority of those encounters are illegal because of the age of the participant, not because of coercion or violence.

That finding was part of a very large comprehensive study, "Online 'Predators' and Their Victims," published February 18 [2008] in the *American Psychologist*. It was based upon three surveys; two were telephone interviews of 3,000 Internet users between the ages of 10 and 17 taken in 2000 and 2005; the third were 612 interviews with law enforcement officials.

Child Sex Abuse Has Declined

Overall, it concluded that hysterical media coverage of isolated events and television programs such *To Catch a Predator* have left a distorted picture of both the scope and nature of this activity. It noted that from 1990 to 2005, reported cases of child sex abuse declined by half and the rates of runaways and pregnancy among teens also declined.

"The reality about Internet-related sex crimes—those in which sex offenders meet juvenile victims online—is different, more complex, and serious but less archetypically frightening than the publicity about these crimes suggests."

"Many victims profess love or close feelings for offenders." . . .

Of the prosecuted cases, 99 percent involved youth 13 to 17, a time of growing independence and exploration, including sexual exploration. The median age for first intercourse is 17.

Romance and sex generally are key factors in those encounters, with sex discussed ahead of time online and anticipated by both parties. "Many victims profess love or close feelings for offenders" and 73 percent of the youth had more than one physical encounter with the same person.

The study concluded "Although a new medium for communication is involved, the non-forcible sex crimes that predominate as offenses against youths only are not particularly new or uncommon."

Targeting Male Youth

Youth with a history of sexual abuse, sexual orientation concerns, and patterns of risk-taking are particularly likely to find sexual encounters online with older partners. About a third of those solicitations came in chatrooms.

Males were the victim in a quarter of all criminal cases. The fact that most met their sexual partner at online sites such as a gay chatroom strongly suggests that being gay or questioning one's sexual orientation is a risk factor.

Study coauthor David Finkelhor, director of the Crimes against Children Research Center, said the survey did not ask the youth to self-identify their sexual orientation. He added, male victims off-line "tend to be younger, particularly 8 to 12 years old."

He made the point, "You don't have to worry about gay sex offenders online; kids are made vulnerable by the fact that they are not able to get good information and support around sexual orientation issues from their family and schools, so they are out there online."

Males were the victim in a quarter of all criminal cases.

The Dangers of Stigmatization

Social stigma, concerns about confidentiality, inability to talk with and often alienation from parents, does lead some gay youth to the Internet, and the potential for exploitation by some adults.

First amendment rights advocate Bill Dobbs said, "There is a great deal of hysteria around youth sexuality, and the Internet just inflames the issue." He stressed the need to differentiate between prepubescent kids and teens "who may not be adults but are not children."

"It is an age-old story, teens on a journey of life and getting around their parents." He stressed the need for society in general to become more educated and accepting of a spectrum of sexual orientations.

8

Cyberbullying Magnifies Social Injustices

Warren Blumenfeld

Warren Blumenfeld specializes in multicultural and international curriculum studies and lesbian, gay, bisexual, transgender, and queer studies. He is coeditor of Investigating Christian Privilege and Religious Oppression in the United States; *coauthor of* Looking at Gay and Lesbian Life; *and coresearcher & coauthor of* 2010 State of Higher Education for Lesbian, Gay, Bisexual, and Transgender People.

Bullying and harassment have always been problems for students who were perceived as different or as outsiders, but the rise of the Internet has provided bullies with an array of new and more efficient tools. To protect gay and lesbian college students, who are often the target of slander and harassment, and to ensure that they can pursue their academic goals safely, faculty, staff, and administrators at campuses nationwide need to work together and provide a safe environment.

Friends described Tyler Clementi as a gentle, kind, and sensitive person who was an accomplished violinist at an early age. Tyler was awarded a music scholarship at the prestigious Rutgers University, and he was looking forward to his four years at Rutgers and to a shining career. On September 22, [2010] however, that great potential ended when Tyler took his life by jumping off the George Washington Bridge. He was only 18 years old.

Tyler's roommate, Dharum Ravi, and another Rutgers student, Molly Wei, both 18 years of age, face charges of invasion of privacy for allegedly tormenting Tyler by using a webcam to secretly record (and live stream on the internet) Tyler engaging in sexual activities in his room with another male student. Dharum tweeted to the over 150 of his followers: "I saw him making out with a dude." And then more recently, "Anyone with iChat, I dare you to video chat me between the hours of 9:30 and 12. Yes, it's happening again!"

Cyberbullying involves information and communication technologies such as Internet web sites, e-mail, chat rooms, mobile phone and pager text messaging, and instant messaging.

Cyberbullying Is on the Rise

While bullying and harassment have long been problems for young people in our nation's schools at every level, the advent of advanced information and communication technologies have now allowed this abusive and destructive practice to extend to virtually all aspects of a person's life.

What has come to be called "cyberbullying," like "face-to-face bullying" (also termed "real life" bullying), involves deliberate and repeated aggressive and hostile behaviors by an individual or group of individuals intended to humiliate, harm, and control another individual or group of individuals of lesser power or social status. Cyberbullying involves information and communication technologies such as Internet web sites, e-mail, chat rooms, mobile phone and pager text messaging, and instant messaging. Cyberbullying has increased exponentially as new technologies are released.

Our study, *2010 State of Higher Education for Lesbian, Gay, Bisexual, and Transgender People*, for Campus Pride included 5,149 participants (LGBT students, faculty, staff, and administrators) representing over 2,000 campuses in all 50 states. We discovered that LGBT students, faculty, and staff remain at significantly higher risk, compared with their heterosexual and gender conforming counterparts, for harassment on our colleges and universities. Participants attending unwelcoming and "hostile" campuses reported lowered interest in remaining at their current campuses and discouraged future students from attending. They also experienced lower educational outcomes and more negative identity development issues of self esteem, and emotional, mental, and physical health.

The majority of participants discussed the overt acts, as well as the subtle microaggressions (as one participant termed, the "death by a thousand tiny cuts") creating an uncomfortable and emotionally and physically unsafe environment.

Harrassment Online Is Common

Cyberbullying appeared among the various forms of harassment and intimidation experienced by participants in our study. According to one participant who defines herself as a lesbian, "Mostly people say some offensive things on an anonymous internet forum linked to our campus. There was also an incident recently in which a professor of color here was racially profiled by our Public Safety."

Faculty, staff, and administrators have chosen colleges and universities as their workplaces to practice their craft. All have a right to live, learn, and work at institutions that not only are welcoming but are also actively working to ensure their emotional and physical safety.

Participants also warned that a popular (now defunct) website, "Juicycampus.com," is the worst thing that has EVER happened to our college campuses. Creators of this website publicize it as "....synonymous with college gossip, and is more popular than ... could have ever expected. We've expanded to more than 500 campuses across the US, and have more than a million unique visitors coming to the site every month."

For students; colleges and universities serve as their homes away from home. Faculty, staff, and administrators have chosen colleges and universities as their workplaces to practice their craft. All have a right to live, learn, and work at institutions that not only are welcoming but are also actively working to ensure their emotional and physical safety.

Our comprehensive research has conclusively exposed the inequities, and the possible best practices we propose have shown proven results. Though it is unfortunately too late to prevent Tyler Clementi's agony and suffering at the hands of his tormentors, we encourage all schools to expand their efforts and to appreciatively raise the discourse in working to secure the safety and the equity for all people, including our LGBTQ students, faculty, staff, and administrators. In this way, colleges and universities may more fully reach their mandate of providing the best quality education and working environment for all members of the campus community.

9

Cyberstalking Can Be a Threat to Anyone

Karen McVeigh

Karen McVeigh is a senior news reporter for the Guardian *(UK). Before that, she wrote for the* Times *following a five-year stint as the* Scotsman's *London correspondent.*

Long believed to be the product of hysteric minds or an urban legend, cyberstalking is now more prevalent than physical harassment. Surprisingly, 40 percent of the victims are men, and the consequences of cyberstalking can be enormous. In a world that is globally connected, anyone with a grudge can disseminate victims' personal information and spread lies about them via the Internet. From spurned lovers to complete strangers, cyberstalkers can destroy a person's reputation, cause serious harm in the workplace with false accusations, and pose a threat to families. However, law enforcement has not yet caught up with the new development, and the punishment often fails to match the severity of the crime. More stringent laws are needed to fight online harassment and protect its victims.

Cyberstalking is now more common than physical harassment, according to new figures due to be released next week, with many victims finding themselves pursued by complete strangers online.

The first study of its kind to look at the extent and effect of cyberstalking, taking in social networking sites, email and mobile phones, has revealed the profile of perpetrators to be radically different from those who pursue victims face-to-face. Victims surveyed by Echo (Electronic Communication Harassment Observation), at Bedford University, reported that their harassers were more likely to be a complete stranger or a casual acquaintance than a former partner.

Another major finding was that nearly 40% of cyberstalking victims are men. Past studies have identified women as much more at risk from face-to-face stalking.

Most of the victims surveyed were aged 20 to 39, although ages ranged from 14 to 74, with teenagers reporting social networking sites as the environment in which they were most likely to be harassed.

Taking Cyberstalking Seriously

Dr Emma Short, psychologist and co-author of the study, launched last September [2010] with the backing of the Crown Prosecution Service, said the crime was not taken as seriously as it should be: "There is a lack of understanding of the impact of this behaviour. One of the biggest questions was, 'Is there psychological harm?' Worryingly, a third experienced this. Not just stress, but a clinical record of psychological harm.

[N]early 40% of cyberstalking victims are men.

"There have been threats to kill. They give the impression that they know where their victims live and can get at them physically. There is a lot of damage to or loss of reputation, people being compromised by false allegations. I spoke to a teacher who was followed through chat rooms and the net by someone claiming to have met him through a child porn site. He had a very supportive head but it went on for several years. He never found out who or what their intention was."

Another victim was bombarded with vivid images of violent rape. It is often unclear what the stalker aims to get out of it, other than causing "misery and distress", she said.

The pattern of harassment is different between male and female victims, she said, with men targeted by strangers more than women. Around 37% of men were stalked by a stranger, compared with 23% of women. Only 4% reported being stalked by a former partner, compared with victims of face-to-face stalking, where around half are former partners, according to Echo.

Stalked by Complete Strangers

The largest category of all victims where the perpetrator was a stranger did not know where they had come from, how they were targeted and never found [out who pursued them, according to the survey]. One in five said the offender targeted them via social networking sites and 16% via blogging forums. Only 4% came from online dating.

Short, who surveyed 250 victims though a questionnaire, said while it is clear that a third of all victims reported clinically recognised symptoms of PTSD [posttraumatic stress disorder], men and women often reacted differently. "For women the fear is of physical violence to themselves and then to their families or children. For men, they are afraid of damage to their reputation.

"The population who harass online are different to the population already understood as harassers by the police and the legislators, so the risks are unclear." . . .

The British Crime Survey 2006 estimates up to 5 million people experience stalking each year, but there are no official statistics on the percentage cyberstalked.

Last week MPs [Members of Parliament] called for an overhaul in the laws governing such crimes, so that both stalking and cyberstalking is legally defined. The Protection from Harassment Act 1997, the law most used to deal with stalking, has not been updated since the explosion of social media, and does not include online stalking.

The Need for New Legislation

At the launch of a parliamentary campaign on the issue, most victims reported that they were unable to get the police to take it seriously; that police found it extremely difficult to gather evidence or were met with a lack of understanding of how best to use the law. . . .

The British Crime Survey 2006 estimates up to 5 million people experience stalking each year, but there are no official statistics on the percentage cyberstalked.

Harry Fletcher of Napo, the probation [officers'] union, said that areas such as stalking through social networking sites and the use of the *internet* to damage reputations were poorly understood by police and not properly defined in law. It is often difficult to get information from internet service providers and proving attribution can be difficult as stalkers have multiple untraceable means of accessing the internet.

Fletcher called for a change in the law to "catch up with technology". He said: "There needs to be training for police and probation into the nature of stalking, the nature of stalking behaviour and how to investigate, particularly internet crimes."

The Real Horror of Being Stalked

It started with a notice on an online bulletin board he knew Joanne would see: her name, her husband's name, their address, email and telephone number. Then, to show he was watching, small details about her family would appear—updates her children had posted on their Facebook sites, with comments such as "X doesn't seem to be very happy today".

A series of false allegations followed. That Joanne and her husband were paedophiles who had sold their daughter to him for sex; that Joanne was a drug dealer and had been involved in criminal activities at work.

The harassment consumed Joanne, 47, and her family, but police failed to take it seriously, she says. "It was in the hands of a community support officer. They just thought I was a hysterical woman. He put us through hell. It was terrifying. One Monday I got up and I couldn't do anything but cry. I thought he was going to kill me."

They knew who he was, a casual acquaintance with a grudge, but it was only after attacks on their car began, causing £3,000 of damage, that he was arrested and charged with harassment, criminal damage and falsifying an alibi. The harassment charge was dropped in a plea bargain and he was sentenced to 200 hours' community service plus costs for criminal damage.

"One Monday I got up and I couldn't do anything but cry. I thought he was going to kill me."

Joanne wants a "more robust law" so that stalkers can be convicted and punished appropriately. "Otherwise people like him will continue to be allowed to make people's lives a misery."

10

Increasingly, Men Are Becoming the Targets of Cyberstalkers

Yair Cohen

Yair Cohen is a UK online defamation and Internet solicitor. He is one of the first lawyers in the United Kingdom to have obtained court injunctions against Google, YouTube, and other main Internet service providers to force these companies to remove defamatory content from their blogs and websites.

The Internet, with its possibilities to connect strangers worldwide, has also created a new danger for men who like to chat online and see chat rooms as a way to get to know women. While the grooming of boys and girls by older predators has garnered national attention, the grooming of men by predator women has been overlooked. Yet an increasing number of men are approached by women online and moved from chat rooms to private communication and—with promises of sex or love— made to expose themselves in front of webcams. The predators record these sessions and later upload them to websites with names and addresses of their victims, and often accompanied by false allegations that the men are pedophiles or child molesters. Once such videos have been disseminated, it is nearly impossible to take them down and ensure they will not resurface. What might have started as harmless online flirtation can ruin men's reputations and careers.

Yair Cohen, "Grooming of Men on the Internet. Seriously . . . ," *Internet Law Expert* (UK), April 9, 2011. www.internetlawexpert.co.uk. Copyright © 2011 by Yair Cohen. All rights reserved. Reproduced by permission.

I am sorry to be indiscreet about this sensitive subject but it looks as if this terrible matter is starting to become an issue for a growing number of men of all different economic and academic backgrounds, who get caught in what appears to be a sting operation which could potentially scar them for life. I have seen families falling apart, and men having to move to a different town and even acquire a new identity.

Chances are that this is the first time you are hearing about this issue and that what is to follow as you read on has no direct relevance to you at all. In fact, you might even be a woman and this story is about men being groomed online.

A Growing Problem

Later on, you will see why we have decided to make all our clients and colleagues aware of this terrible issue and if, as I expect, this subject is completely foreign to you, please do pass this note to other men you know and care about. You could be doing them a big favour.

Many men whether rich or poor, married or single take part in chatting and in most cases quite innocently.

We hear a lot about young girls being groomed on the internet by older men. This is of course one of the most disturbing subjects concerning internet use. What we do not hear about however, and what you are just about to discover as you read on, is the ease by which and the terrible consequences for men, of all ages, [are] being groomed by women over the internet, having their photos, videos and personal details stolen and then spread over websites of a certain nature all over the world.

In short, there are some free forums on the internet for people to chat about anything and everything. Naturally these forums tend to be regarded as 'meeting places' where people talk to strangers, exchange ideas and look for relationships, virtual or otherwise. One of these forums is called Chatabox. You can join up for free and then, you can start chatting immediately. You can chat to almost anyone who is online at the time. I am not singling out Chatabox and I do not suggest the website owners are doing anything wrong. There are other similar websites which offer free chat and Chatabox is a very popular one and all those who came to me for advice following their horrific experience which I will describe below, have mentioned Chatabox as the place where their nightmare started.

Many men whether rich or poor, married or single take part in chatting and in most cases quite innocently. It is just another way for many to relax from the day's chores and have a relaxing conversation with other online chatters. It is normally a friendly place which at times, as you will find out, can become very dangerous indeed.

The Growing Danger of Predators

What many of these men don't realise is that there are some dangerous predators out there, ready to eat them alive. Not literally but also not very far from that.

The predator women do not look for perverts or men who are regular visitors to certain type of websites as these men tend to be far more suspicious and much more discrete. They hunt for an easy prey instead.

These dangerous predators I am talking about are women who have conspired to groom men and take them away from the chat site, where their identity can be revealed quite easily, to a private chat programme such as MSN Messenger, AOL Messenger or Yahoo Messenger, where they intend to seduce their victims into performing compromising acts, totally naked, in front of a webcam. Unbeknownst to their victims, the predator will capture the video, save it to their computer, edit it and then post it on hundreds of websites, the nature of which is obvious.

But there is still worse to come.

The way the operation appears to be working is this: initially the woman will hunt for her victim. She will try several men before finding one who appears to be naïve so far as internet usage is concerned. The predator women do not look for perverts or men who are regular visitors to certain type of websites as these men tend to be far more suspicious and much more discrete. They hunt for an easy prey instead.

Hunting for Naïve Users

Their typical victim will be a school teacher, a dentist or a police officer. The initial conversation will be very innocent. It tends to be about work, family, location and so on. Suspecting of nothing, the victim will often divulge their children's names and the name of the company they work for. Naturally, once they have given this sort of information, the men become even more trusting. It is a psychological thing that sharing personal information accelerates the feelings of trust that we feel about our partner to the conversation.

Then the woman speaks about herself and, surprise surprise, it transpires she and her victim have a lot in common. They both might be a bit lonely, they both could have some marital difficulties to resolve and they both are likely to be craving for love and affection. Neither of them of course will contemplate having an extra marital affair mainly because of their loyalty to their family. At the suggestion of the woman predator, the conversation will then move to a private chat programme such as Yahoo Messenger or MSN Messenger. This will break the 'continuity of evidence'. Whilst on the public chat, the parties can relatively easily be traced through their account registration details. This will be almost an impossible task with a private chat programme. The move from one chat programme to another will also break the link between the grooming and the shocking action which will follow.

The conversation will continue on the private chat programme and will turn more and more personal until it becomes purely suggestive. Eventually the victim will be encouraged to perform a compromising act on himself on camera so that the predator, whose job is almost done can "watch, participate and enjoy". Once the compromising act is concluded the chat will come to its abrupt end by the predator simply switching off the programme at her end.

What happens next is very interesting and is probably beyond most people's comprehension.

Following the video conversation which was fully recorded by the female predator onto her computer, she will compile several video clips and will give them titles such as

---

The victim will wake up in the morning to a new reality. He will first find an interesting email in his mail box from an unknown email address with a short note by his predator and a video attachment.

'John Smith From 91 Cleveland Lane Road, London, A GP [General Practitioner] and Child Molester Fxxxg Himself In Front of School Children' as well as other similarly colourful commentary.

She will then post these videos on to several websites including YouTube and distribute them to countless other websites all over the world.

Being Exposed and Smeared Online

The victim will wake up in the morning to a new reality. He will first find an interesting email in his mail box from an unknown email address with a short note by his predator and a video attachment.

Having watched the horrific video, most victims will immediately carry out an internet search against their own name only to discover that their worst fears have been materialised. By this time, the links which contain the videos have gathered so much popularity, especially following their distribution to the entire world by blogs and emails, that sometimes almost the entire first page of a Google search could be full of links to these videos, each time with a different title and commentary.

A total nightmare. If the victim is married, he will now need to speak to his wife and explain how he allowed this situation to happen. This you can imagine would be quite a challenging task in itself. It could be a matter of time before his employers will find out, the kids, other family members, the neighbours, business associates or even some thugs who would believe that he is really a child molester or a paedophile.

At this stage the victims normally seek legal advice. They want to know what would happen if or rather when certain people discover these videos, in particular their employers. With most employers, it is a sackable offence to bring their organisation into disrepute. Naturally, when we speak to the victims, many of them are in a state of extreme shock.

Before we deal with any other issue which troubles them, we give priority to the immediate removal of the videos from the several video hosting websites. This could be done fairly quickly but of course the sooner we act the better because as time goes by, the number of links tend to increase and so does the popularity of the videos, as well as the number of people who copy these videos onto their personal computer and could potentially redistribute them in the future. The removal of these videos does not however guarantee that they will not reappear in the future.

The Removal of Movies Can Be Difficult

It is important that the victims sign up for a monitoring system which operates 24/7 to give early warnings of any future distribution of their compromising videos. Potentially, these videos can reappear on the internet at any time in the years to come. In any event, with the internet, it is all about speed speed speed so the priority is to have these videos removed from video hosts sites as quickly as possible.

I cannot tell for sure what is the precise motive behind the action of the predator woman, but having lately seen so many of these cases I have no doubt that there is indeed a system behind this operation and I am almost convinced that the female predators do this for money.

Legally, little can be done to go back in time.

In legal terms, all the victims in such cases have a cause of action in the courts, particularly for breach of privacy. Although legal action could eventually lead us to the predators' identity this would be very costly and will bring further unwanted attention to the matter, and with it, further reputational damage to the victims. In cases such as this, any publicity is bad publicity. The police are unlikely to be willing or able to intervene, mainly because of lack or resources and due to the fact that victims choose not to lodge a formal complaint.

I will leave it for your imagination to picture the devastation this could cause someone. I have seen male victims changing their name and moving to a different town in order to avoid detection. I also witnessed families falling apart and men feeling suicidal following their involvement as victims in this sting.

Education Is More Helpful than Seeking Retribution

Legally, little can be done to go back in time. No level of compensation will persuade any man in his right mind to pursue such a matter through the courts. Sometimes keeping your head down is the best advice to follow.

What is left is for us to spread the word, inform the public and educate people to be more vigilant whilst chatting on the internet. You have to remember that the vast majority of the men who find their lives falling apart as a result of being groomed, are innocent victims who were perhaps guilty of being naïve or even a bit reckless, but are certainly not sexual offenders or perverts and do not deserve the potential life sentence which they may have to serve day in and day out. . . .

I am not condoning the use of internet chats by married men to look for virtual extra marital affairs. This is a subject of another conversation. However, everyone would agree that it is important to educate both adults and children about some of the dangers of internet chat. These are the dark sides of our new global society and they are not likely to simply disappear. It is only by having people such as yourself passing on this information to others that we can make the internet a safer place for both ourselves and to the next generation.

11

Common Sense Is Needed to Face the Dangers of Online Dating Sites

Single City Guy

The Single City Guy *blog is written by an anonymous New York City resident.*

The case of a woman who sued Match.com for damages follow-ing a sexual assault by a man, who was a registered sex offender, has raised the issue of liability for such websites. Can these sites can be held responsible for the actions of their members, and do they need to screen their databases for criminal records? Yet while dating sites should do their best to ensure customers' safety, they should not invade people's privacy. The danger of misuse of personal data outweighs the potential benefits of invasive screen-ings. In the end, while safe dating zones might be established to reduce the risk of assault, people must take personal responsibil-ity for their own safety.

The debate about the responsibilities of websites has re-cently [April 2011] arisen from the sexual assault of a Californian woman by a guy she met through a dating web-site. [It was reported], that after the second date, with some-one she met from Match.com, the man followed her home and sexually assaulted her. The man had been previously clas-sified as a sexual offender. The woman, thru a lawsuit, is plac-ing blame at Match.com for not protecting her from sexual offenders, and her lawyer indicates that dating websites should scan its users against a the sex-offenders database and remove offenders from the site. This case is another chapter of sex-offenders on online websites, and revisits some of the concerns when sexual offenders were found on social networking websites (i.e. MySpace, when popular; and Facebook.) There are differences between the two incidents. The concern with social networking sites, are that sexual offenders will target minors. It's such a hot-button issue legislation was drafted, barring sex offenders from social networking sites.

With this topic, the debate, shifts in a different direction. Dating websites, like Match.com, are for adults, with the assumption that adults will be responsible for their own actions. Creating a system where dating websites screen for sexual offenders has several convoluted issues. It delves into the issue of responsibility; if a website's sole purpose is to play as match maker, where does their responsibility begin and end? . . .

Before furthering the discussion, I want to mention that Single City Guy does [have] an affiliation with Match.com. A few months ago, they have provided a free account to their services for review purposes. However, Match.com, or its affiliated websites and partners do not have control of any content that appears on this blog. Which means, I hold every right to criticize them (if I choose). I also work in the tech industry and have certain views of privacy, and ethical standards about technology. What adds to the complexity is, the interactions with today's social media, lends ourselves to show things we wouldn't if a Facebook or Foursquare didn't exist. So the question about sex offenders, and dating websites, and the ramifications it has, is very important. The fallout from this lawsuit, and larger discussions to come, will be things that affect our online lives. . . .

The Profile of a Sex Offender

The definition for a sex offender is broader than you may think. While it includes rapists and child molesters, it also includes those who have violated a law that includes sex as part its classification. In some states, sexting is a sex offense. Other states, the difference in age could cause someone to be classified as a sex offender. In Green Bay, a 17 year-old, who is sexually active with a 16 year-old could be arrested and be classified as a sex offender. In under 7 years, that 17-year-old will be 24, and most likely online dating. There are other ways that a person can be classified as a sex offender, such as a second prostitution conviction.

To further examine the grey area of being classified as a sex offender, consider Lawrence Taylor, who is now a registered sex offender. His offense, was having sex with an underage prostitute, who he didn't know was under age. While he's registered as a low-level sex offender (level 1), he has to remain registered for 20 years. It's hard to decide who are the sex offenders because of circumstance, or who are the bad guys. I don't think rapists and child molesters should use websites where they could do harm. However, there is a distinction from a rapist, and a teenager who was dating someone younger, when he turned 18. That kid is now 21, and still considered a sex offender. . . .

In Green Bay, a 17 year-old who is sexually active with a 16 year-old could be arrested and be classified as a sex offender.

Dating Websites and Anti-Sex Offender Policy

I want to strongly believe dating websites should check their users for previous sexual offenses. While it may sound logical, performing that policy isn't that simple. The first issue to tackle is the classification of a sex offender. As I've explained above, there are cases where those classified as sex offenders due to circumstance, and not of criminal standing. Then, there's the question of enacting such a system. While it's easy to say, that users of a website should have their names cross referenced with the sex offender database; what needs to be considered is the process that may entail. A website could automatically scan names and addresses, but mistaken identities will arise. If there's two people named "John Smith" in an area, and one of them is a sex offender, there's the possibility that both John Smith's will be flagged as sex offenders. One of them will be automatically labeled as something he isn't.

A dating website may know people's personality types, preference in their matches, or how often they search for a match; but that information can't predict how a person will act in a relationship.

The largest issue is privacy. Especially, how are dating websites determining if you're a sex offender or not, and what other information are they using to possibly prevent you from using their services? It would concern me if a dating website started to background check its users. If I had a warrant out for my arrest, because of an unpaid parking ticket, would that favor negatively against me? [If I were] a sex offender, I would be technically classified as a criminal. If my account was flagged with criminal status, what would happen to me next? Clearly, someone who didn't pay a parking ticket isn't a murderer, but performing a background check because I want to use a dating website, will invade my privacy. They also shouldn't cross reference my name or payment information against databases to decide if I'm qualified to use a website. It reeks of a corporation intruding on my privacy.

Also consider that dating websites typically don't ask for a lot of information during their sign-up process. While you may have to fill out a profile, dating websites don't ask for explicit information like addresses, until entering payment information. At best a dating website would get my first and last name, the city or zip code I live in, and my physical traits. Sites like OkCupid, and Plenty Of Fish are free, and have less information about me than Match.com. Personally, I don't feel the need to give them any more information than what they have. I could have also falsified my name and location, and most dating websites use screen names to identify users against each other.

So while I want to say that dating website should have a policy to keep sex offenders from their websites; doing that could severely invade my privacy.

Dating websites have a responsibility to its users to protect them, in the best way possible.

Websites and Their Responsibilities

Many dating websites guarantee dates. They sell themselves as being responsible for matching two unknown people together. If a couple gets married, the website is quick to promote that story as a "success story", due to their website. Logically, it's seen as the dating website was responsible for their marriage. Using this logic, if a crime happens, because the dating website matched two people together, and one has lead a life of crime, then the website is also responsible for that crime. I would like to suggest, both assumptions are wrong.

A dating website may know people's personality types, preference in their matches, or how often they search for a match; but that information can't predict how a person will act in a relationship. The algorithm for matching people may show great matches, but once in the room life experiences, personality traits, and circumstances can may make them incompatible. Dating websites do not know if two people will get married, or will break up. Often, when a dating website praises a success story, they don't mention the amount of time, or dates it took to find that person. Rarely do two recent matches end up in marriage. It takes a few matches.

Just because two people met through a dating website, doesn't mean the website is responsible for their marriage. It merely put those two people in the same room. When conflicts in the relation happen, the dating website doesn't help with the conflict; the reasons blogs, magazines, and therapists exists. The only thing a dating website does, is say "I've found some new matches for you." While it's easy to say that a dating website is responsible for a marriage, the truth is, it's only responsible for placing two people it believes are compatible, in touch with one another. The only way a dating website can be held responsible for a relationship, is if the same websites are held responsible for the breakup's, the divorces, and those who cheat. If a website like Ashley Madison is the blame for failures of a relationship, it must also be blamed for the successes of a relationship.

A dating website isn't responsible for your interactions on a date. If they get drunk and throw up on your dress, a dating website doesn't owe you a new dress. Sadly to say, I believe the same is true for a crime. If someone gets mugged, raped, or abused, because they met through a dating website, the website shouldn't be responsible for those actions. Why? A dating website merely presents a profile of a person that it thinks you will like. It doesn't force you to communicate with them, it doesn't force you to continue communicating with them, and it doesn't force you to go on a second date with them. It only connects you with another person. It's a choice whether to accept or deny the connection. . . .

What Dating Websites Can Do to Protect Their Users

With the arguments I've made above, it seems as if dating websites are off the hook. But they aren't. Dating websites have a responsibility to its users to protect them, in the best way possible. Often this means, keeping their personal information safe, so that others cannot view them. There's more than just keeping credit card numbers, photos and names under lock and key, there's a responsibility for making sure its users are safe. Most dating websites have a "safe dating tip" section, where members could read, and learn about safety. I believe dating websites could do a bit more than simply publish a safety guideline for everyone to follow. The same way large marketing campaigns are created for selling a product, there could be marketing campaigns to inform the public of online dating safety. Even then, I believe there's more they can do.

While websites could, and should do more, there's a line that needs to be respected. That of privacy and ethics.

In the case of Match.com being sued, the guy attacked the woman after following her home, after the second date. There isn't a website that could prevent against that situation. The guy seemed safe enough to go on a second date with, and took the time and effort to follow her back to her home. There's a planning, and a method to creeps like that, that are rarely prevented by merely removing them from a website. There are proactive measures a person must undertake to protect themselves.

Safe Dating Zones

With that said, there could be some middle ground when it comes to safety. Websites should partner with locations to create "safe dating zones" or pair with taxi companies to give safe travel to and from their dating destinations. These actions may not prevent a crime, like what happened to this Californian woman, but it can help find the man, catch him quicker, and offer other safeguards to make sure that people are meeting in safe places and returning home safely. There's more innovation that can ... [improve] the system, but it goes beyond the control of the website. The same way sex offenders need to register their location, they could register their e-mail addresses. This list can be provided as a measure to block membership (as most websites use e-mails as part of their registration). While it's personal, it's information everyone is willing to provide, to ensure safety.

While websites could, and should do more, there's a line that needs to be respected. That of privacy and ethics. When two adults meet, through a dating website, they are responsible for their actions. What happens on that date isn't the responsibly of any service. They are also responsible for their own safety and common sense. Situations, like the one in California, does raise a few questions of what else can be done to help protect . . . [dating site] members. While the situation isn't common, I believe there are steps that dating websites and their users could [take] to be safer.

Organizations to Contact

The editors have compiled the following list of organizations concerned with the issues debated in this book. The descriptions are derived from materials provided by the organizations. All have publications or information available for interested readers. The list was compiled on the date of publication of the present volume: names, addresses, phone and fax numbers, and e-mail and Internet addresses may change. Be aware that many organizations take several weeks or longer to respond to inquiries, so allow as much time as possible.

Beatbullying
+44 (0)20 8771-3377 • Fax: +44 (0)20 8771-8550
e-mail: info@beatbullying.org
website: www.beatbullying.org

Beatbullying works with children and teenagers across the UK to provide important opportunities to change their lives and outlook positively. In particular, the organization works with those so deeply affected by bullying that they fear going to school. Beatbullying also seeks to effect change in bullies' behavior, working with them to take responsibility and a sense of ownership over their actions. Videos, news, and "lesson plans," like the "Friendship and Peer Pressure Lesson Plan" are available online.

Childnet International
Studio 14 Brockley Cross Business Centre, London   SE4 2PD
+44 (0)20 7639-6967 • Fax: +44 (0)20 7639-7027
e-mail: info@childnet.com
website: www.childnet.com

The Childnet International website gives Internet safety advice and links for children, teenagers, parents, and teachers. The organization is dedicated to helping young people to use the Internet constructively and showcase quality content. Policy papers and annual reviews are available online.

ConnectSafely

website: www.connectsafely.org

ConnectSafely is a forum for parents, teens, educators, and advocates designed to give teens and parents a voice in the public discussion about youth online safety. The site offers tips, as well as other resources, for safe social networking.

Cyberbully411

website: www.cyberbully411.org

Cyberbully411 provides resources and opportunities for discussion and sharing for teenagers who want to know more about—or have been victims of—online harassment. The website was created by the nonprofit Internet Solutions for Kids, Inc., and invites teenagers to share their stories or download tips and information on cyberbullying, depression, and other relevant topics.

Federal Trade Commission (FTC)

600 Pennsylvania Avenue, NW, Washington, DC   20580
(202) 326-2222
website: www.ftc.gov

The FTC deals with issues of the everyday economic life. It is the only federal agency with both consumer protection and competition jurisdiction. The FTC strives to enforce laws and regulations and to advance consumers' interests by sharing its expertise with federal and state legislatures and US and international government agencies. Publications about online safety and cyber crime can be downloaded from its website.

GetNetWise

e-mail: cmatsuda@neted.org
website: www.getnetwise.org

GetNetWise is a public service provided by Internet industry corporations and public interest organizations to help Internet users experience safe online research and entertainment. The

GetNetWise coalition wants users to make informed decisions about their and their family's use of the Internet. The organization provides articles on spam and kids' safety on its website.

Institute for Responsible Online and Cell Phone Communication (I.R.O.C.2)

The Institute for Responsible Online
  and Cell-Phone Communication
Mount Laurel, NJ   08054-9998
(877) 295-2005
website: www.iroc2.org

I.R.O.C.2 is a nonprofit organization advocating for digital responsibility, safety, and awareness. It endorses the development and safe use of all digital devices (e.g., digital cameras, cell phones, computers, Internet, video cams, web cameras, etc.) and the World Wide Web. The organization's creation is based on the fact that many individuals are not aware of the short- and long-term consequences of their own actions when utilizing digital technologies. Articles on sextcasting and the organization's "Cyber General" are available online.

Internet Keep Safe Coalition

1401 K Street N.W., Suite 600, Washington, DC   20005
(202) 587-5583 • Fax: (202) 737-4097
e-mail: info@iKeepSafe.org
website: www.iKeepSafe.org

iKeepSafe.org—which features Faux Paw the Techno Cat—is a coalition of 49 governors/first spouses, law enforcement, the American Medical Association, the American Academy of Pediatrics, and other associations dedicated to helping parents, educators, and caregivers by providing information and guidelines to teach children the safe use of technology.

National Center for Missing & Exploited Children (NCMEC)

Charles B. Wang International Children's Building
Alexandria, Virginia   22314-3175

(703) 224-2150 • Fax: (703) 224-2122
website: www.ncmec.org

The NCMEC's mission is to help prevent child abduction and sexual exploitation. The organization assists in finding missing children and supports victims of child abduction and sexual exploitation. Its website provides articles on sexual exploitation, sex offenders, and how to guard against online predators.

OnGuard Online

e-mail: OnGuardOnline@ftc.gov
website: Onguardonline.gov

OnGuardOnline.gov provides tips from the federal government and the technology industry to help consumers be on guard against Internet fraud, secure computers, and protect personal information. The website offers information and games to test individuals' cyber savviness.

Wired Safety

website: www.wiredsafety.org

WiredSafety.org is an Internet safety and help group. It provides educational material, news, assistance, and awareness on all aspects of cybercrime and abuse, privacy, security, and responsible technology use. It is also the parent group of Teenangels.org, FBI-trained teens and preteens who promote Internet safety.

Bibliography

Books

Tomi Ahonen

Mobile as 7th of the Mass Media: Cellphone, Cameraphone, iPhone, Smartphone. London (UK): futuretext, 2008.

Yaman Akdeniz

Internet Child Pornography and the Law: National and International Responses. Farnham, UK: Ashgate, 2008.

Julia Angwin

Stealing MySpace: The Battle to Control the Most Popular Website in America. New York: Random House, 2009.

Debra Baartz

Australians, the Internet and Technology-enabled Child Sex Abuse: A Statistical Profile. Australian Federal Police, 2008.

Jack Balkin et al., eds.

Cybercrime: Digital Cops in a Networked Environment. New York: New York University Press, 2006.

Naomi Baron

Always On: Language in an Online and Mobile World. Oxford, United Kingdom: Oxford University Press, 2010.

Council of Europe

Protecting Children from Sexual Violence: A Comprehensive Approach. Strasbourg Cedex: Council of Europe Publishing, 2010.

Marcus Erooga and Helen Masson, eds. — *Children and Young People Who Sexually Abuse Others: Challenges and Responses.* London: Routledge, 2006.

Charles Ess — *Digital Media Ethics: Digital Media and Society.* Cambridge, United Kingdom: Polity, 2009.

Stefan Fafinski — *Computer Misuse: Response, Regulation and the Law.* Cullompton, United Kingdom: Willan, 2009.

Anastasia Goodstein — *Totally Wired: What Teens and Tweens Are Really Doing Online.* New York: St. Martin's Griffin, 2007.

Peter Grabosky — *Electronic Crime.* Princeton, NJ: Prentice Hall, 2006.

Dennis Howitt and Kerry Sheldon — *Sex Offenders and the Internet.* New York: John Wiley & Sons, 2007.

James Michael Lampinen and Kathy Sexton-Radek — *Protecting Children from Violence: Evidence-based Interventions.* New York: Psychology Press, 2010.

Samuel McQuade, ed. — *Understanding and Managing Cybercrime.* Boston, Mass.: Allyn & Bacon, 2006.

Samuel McQuade III, James Colt, and Nancy Meyer — *Cyber Bullying: Protecting Kids and Adults from Online Bullies.* New York: Praeger, 2009

Laura Saba

Textual Intercourse: Dating and Relating in a Cellular World. Philadeplhia, PA: Running Press, 2009.

Mike Sullivan

Online Predators. Longwood, FL: Xulon Books, 2008.

Ian Walden

Computer Crimes and Digital Investigations. Oxford, United Kingdom: Oxford University Press, 2007.

David Wall

Cybercrimes: The Transformation of Crime in the Information Age. Cambridge, United Kingdom: Polity, 2007.

Matthew Williams

Virtually Criminal: Crime, Deviance and Regulation Online. London: Routledge, 2006.

Majid Yar

Cybercrime and Society. London: Sage, 2006.

Periodicals and Internet Sources

Michael Bourke, and Andres Hernandez

"The 'Butner Study' Redux: A Report of the Incidence of Hands-on Child Victimization by Child Pornography Offenders." *Journal of Family Violence*, 2009.

Bruce Bower

"Internet Seduction: Online Sex Offenders Prey on At-Risk Teens," *Science News*, February 23, 2008.

Bruce Bower — "Growing Up Online: Young People Jump Headfirst into the Internet's World," *Science News*, June 17, 2006.

Christian Science Monitor — "'Sexting' Overreach," April 28, 2009.

Curriculum Review — "Teens Share Sexually Explicit Messages: Simple Rebellion or Dangerous Behavior?" May 2009.

Maryjoy Duncan — "The Serious Implications of 'Sexting'" *El Chicano Weekly*, April 22, 2010.

Florida Parishes Bureau — "Loranger Teen Booked in Threats to Harm Other Teen, Cyberstalking," *Capital City Press*, July 12, 2007.

Joshua Herman — "Sexting: It's No Joke, It's a Crime," *Illinois Bar Journal*, April 1, 2010.

Idaho State Journal — "Should Sexting Be a Crime?" April 4, 2010.

Eric Janus and Emily Polachek — "A Crooked Picture: Re-Framing the Problem of Child Sexual Abuse." *William Mitchell Law Review*, 2009.

Eric S. Janus and R. Prentky — "Sexual Predator Laws: A Two-Decade Retrospective." *Federal Sentencing Reporter*, 2008.

Monica Jones — "Your Child and the Internet: Tips to Keep Them Safe on the Information Superhighway," *Ebony*, March 2006.

Maureen Macfarlane — "Misbehavior in Cyberspace: The Rise in Social Networking Sites and Chat Rooms Intermingles Free Expression and Student Safety in Cyberspace," *School Administrator*, October 2007.

The National Campaign to Prevent Teen and Unwanted Pregnancy and CosmoGirl.com. — "Sex and Tech: Results from a Survey of Teen and Young Adults." Washington, DC: National Campaign to Prevent Teen and Unwanted Pregnancy, 2008.

Benjamin Radford — "Predator Panic: A Closer Look," *Skeptical Inquirer*, September 2006.

Christine Rosen — "Virtual Friendship and the New Narcissism," *The New Atlantis*, 2007.

Chiara Sabina, Janis Wolak, and David Finkelhor — "Rapid Communication: The Nature and Dynamics of Internet Pornography Exposure for Youth." *CyberPsychology and Behavior*, 2008.

Brian Solis — "Cultural Voyeurism and Social Media," *Social Media Today*, March 17, 2008.

Washington Times — "School Districts Hope Students Get the Picture about 'Sexting' Dangers," July 23, 2009.

Wales On Sunday (Cardiff, Wales) — "Phone Craze Teens Could Face Child Porn Claims; Sordid Trend of Youngsters 'Sexting' Lewd Images of Themselves on Its Way to Wales," June 7, 2009.

Perry A. Zirkel   "All a Twitter About Sexting: Sexual Content in Text Messages Raises Legal Questions for Schools," *Phi Delta Kappa*, 2009.

Index